JOHN DEWEY'S SOCIAL PHILOSOPHY

Oswald Sobrino

Sobrino Works

CONTENTS

NEW 2022 INTRODUCTION

This book reproduces the original award-winning essay entitled "The Relevance of John Dewey's Social Philosophy." This essay, completed in March 1983, was the first-place winner in the 1983 John Dewey Undergraduate Essay Project sponsored by The Center for Dewey Studies at Southern Illinois University, Carbondale, Illinois. The original manuscript, as a PDF file, is available at:

https://www.academia.edu/2197681/
The_Relevance_of_John_Deweys_Social_Philosophy.

Although I wrote this essay as an undergraduate in the nineteen eighties, the social philosophy of John Dewey remains relevant today in the 21st century as American politics continues to be driven by the conflict between cruel right-wing policies and the continuing quest for social justice and fairness for all. May the ideals of John Dewey, a great American philosopher and educator, inspire others today and in the future, especially in extending the privileges of a small elite to a wider and wider group of educated citizens.

I must also note with gratitude that this essay was possible in the first place due to the excellent and inspiring instruction in American Pragmatism provided by Dr. Sandra B. Rosenthal as a philosophy teacher in the Loyola University New Orleans Honors Program in the early nineteen eighties.

Finally, the essay mentions in passing the Spectator Theory of Knowledge and the Non-Spectator Theory of Knowledge, which are likely unfamiliar terms to many readers. The Spectator Theory of Knowledge is the more traditional view in philosophy in which the human knower "sees" external objects as they are in themselves apart from the knower. The Non-Spectator Theory of Knowledge emphasizes that the human knowers themselves influence what knowledge is derived from external objects. Dewey advocates the Non-Spectator Theory of Knowledge, pioneered by Kant's categories, which matches Dewey's emphasis on the human being immersed in nature learning from interactions with the environment without the traditionally sharper separation between knower and object. Compare "Pragmatism," by Douglas McDermid, *The Internet Encyclopedia of Philosophy,* part 2.d., at https://iep.utm.edu/pragmati/.

(Note: I have reproduced the original essay divided by chapters instead of the original essay sections; hence I now refer to another *chapter,* not to a another *section.* I have also corrected minor typographical or spelling errors and made some format and citation adjustments. Otherwise, the book is identical to the original 1983 essay which can be found, for purposes of comparison, in scanned PDF form at my personal profile in the *Academia.edu* website. The use of "man" and its variants to refer to both male and female remains a feature of the original essay, a feature which I attempt to avoid, when possible, in my own current writing.)

Oswald Sobrino, Ph.D.

ORIGINAL 1983 PREFACE

We are presently in a time of political introspection in America: reflective persons considering our economic problems are increasingly frustrated in their search for a coherent approach that will secure economic well-being for all through our democratic institutions. [Author's note: this essay was written in the early 1980s during the first part of the Reagan administration as conservative economic policies costing the jobs of many were ruthlessly implemented. Subsequent notes and additions to the original essay are also in brackets.] This goal involves us in a dilemma; we are searching for a way to pursue the two ideals of our political tradition: liberty and equality. Increasingly, there is a sense of desperation about the possibility that these two goals can be reconciled, as the dualisms of inflation vs. unemployment, free enterprise vs. planning, and merit vs. social justice continue to stubbornly burden us. Any relevant social thought must enable us to intelligently approach such dualisms—and the more complex dualisms that will arise as our society develops further.

John Dewey wrote and lectured roughly from the time of the Progressive Era at the turn of the [twentieth] century to the time of the New Deal. At this time, American society was facing even more disturbing social problems; for in Dewey's time, the New Deal institutions, that put a floor on any economic decline we presently experience, were matters of fierce debate. But what can a philosopher living in such a different era say to our problems?

Even in his own time, Dewey did not set out to construct

specific solutions for social problems. As a philosopher, John Dewey sought to explore the fundamental factors that lead to intractable dualisms, such as those previously mentioned. Dewey searched for a general explanation for our social dilemmas, and why these dilemmas stubbornly reject the prefabricated solutions of various political factions. Thus, persons reflecting on current social problems can turn to Dewey, not for an ideological framework that will provide a sure path to Zion, but rather for a methodological approach to our thinking about social problems that offers the best way experience has given us to find solutions that work.

Dewey's approach is that of the scientific method of creativity, activity, and test. This approach is the clue that Dewey offers to the problems of a different generation of Americans living in a more complex era in our history. If Mr. Dewey's presentation of his social thought gives us a credible and coherent approach to social problems, then we are foolish not to test it in experience. But before we can test this hypothesis, let us examine its meaning and inquire if it offers any insights different from those produced by the present circus of ideology.

CHAPTER 1: THE EPISTEMIC BACKGROUND TO AN ACTIVIST PHILOSOPHY

Dewey's philosophy has been characterized by philosopher Charles Frankel as a social philosophy since for Dewey "all philosophy was at bottom a social philosophy implicitly or explicitly."[1] Dewey's philosophy is thus ultimately concerned with social problems; and with his characteristic consistency, Dewey endeavors to make all of his writings, including those on epistemology, contribute to his ultimate concern with social problems. Thus, to truly understand Dewey's approach to social problems, analysis must begin with his epistemic views. The ideas that result from his consideration of epistemology and its history will reappear in the approach he adopts when considering social problems.

Thus, an examination that will do justice to the distinctive nature of Dewey's social thought must commence with, at least, a brief presentation of his theory of knowledge in relation to traditional epistemic thought. A recent example illustrates the necessity of understanding Dewey's epistemology before dismissing his social views.

One contemporary political scientist assigns Dewey's social philosophy to an obsolete category of political theory primarily for two reasons. First, Dewey, like other "naïve" theorists of the early twentieth century, is said to have viewed the democratic process as essentially a market process analogous to that of a capitalist market economy.[2] This criticism arises from a fundamental confusion of the pragmatic focus on consequences, as the result of guided and purposeful experimentation, with the uncontrolled and irrational market forces of a capitalist economy. The second criticism by the author portrays Dewey as overlooking the effect of parties in blurring class conflict by reducing government's responsiveness to specific electorates.[3] On the contrary, Dewey recognizes that the basic problem of modern democracy is the lack of an effective public organized for inquiry—a problem that is still with us. Understanding the epistemic foundation of Dewey's social philosophy is probably the most effective way to reduce such confusion as has been illustrated.

The primary problem that Dewey discovers in the Western view of knowledge is that of the separation of thought from practice. In the *Quest for Certainty*, Dewey sought to examine the history of the theory of knowledge in order to explain the emergence and relevance of the contemporary view of knowledge.

As the title of his Gifford Lectures indicates, Dewey sees the quest for certainty as the catalyst for the rise of the epistemic theories of the past. The search for certainty arose from man's existential anxiety. Life was and is a constantly alternating scenario of failure, frustration, and a few glorious moments. In order to preserve the fulfillment and positive value of those glorious moments, men began to value contemplation and thought as a way to preserve a realm of safety for all that was valuable in life. Within this realm these positive values would be safe from the decay of change inherent in activity and would also have a secure position from which to provide meaning and certainty to man's life. Religious beliefs were the first formulations of this realm of certainty: religious myths pointed to a world beyond the ordinary world in which the ultimate meaning and reality of experience resided. The transition from religious myth, such as found in Homer and Hesiod, to philosophic thought as exemplified by the pre-Socratics was a process of purgation. The first philosophers sought explanations, apart from the mystery of deities, in the realm of human reason. In short, the early philosophers replaced the gods with rational principles and ideas that were intelligible—that gave us knowledge rather than fear. The realm of the unchanging that secured the values of life now became the realm of knowledge to which reason gave us access. Most of the various monistic philosophies sought to reduce the complexity of the changing world to the unchanging simplicity of a form of being. By the time of Socrates, the Atomists had already postulated the existence of discrete, unchanging particles underlying reality.

With Plato the view that knowledge is about the unchanging and about what is ultimately real culminates in the Divided Line in which true knowledge comes from the contemplation of the Forms. But now, we must ask about the social ramifications of this epistemic view. The social ramifications involve the resulting views of leisure and activity. Activity is concerned with securing a livelihood from the changing world of experience and is thus associated with the failure and frustration inherent in experience. On the other hand, leisure provides the opportunity for contemplation and meditation that provide true knowledge, not opinion. Thus, knowledge is the domain of those with leisure—the aristocratic elite. It is no accident that the circle of young Athenians that was captivated with Socrates was a circle of young aristocrats. In the modern period, Descartes would produce his *Meditations* isolated in a room in southern Germany. In fact, many of the thinkers of the modern period can be characterized as "gentlemen philosophers." The religious and philosophical split between thought and activity became socially apparent in the prestige accorded to the aristocratic lifestyle of leisure at the expense of the practical activity that in fact sustained the community. The aristocrat became the inhabitant of a higher realm, the laborer the inhabitant of a degenerate realm. Thus, the social cleavages arising from conquest were given metaphysical foundations.

With the rise of Newtonian science, the Greek-Medieval view that ultimate reality consisted of qualitative forms was challenged by the scientific school, reminiscent of the Atomist school, that the unchanging substances that were ultimately real were not qualitative but rather quantitative. The separation between thought and activity was maintained; but a problem arose—the alienation of man from nature. As long as nature was seen as a degenerate reflection of real qualitative Forms, nature could still be seen as qualitative, although inferior. But with the rise of modern science, a metaphysical dualism between the realm of mind and values and the realm of nature and extension resulted. The split between thought and activity led to the split between man and his environment. The Rationalism of Descartes sought the reconciliation of these two realms in the person of an undeceiving God. But the empiricist reaction to rationalism culminated in Humeian skepticism that appropriated and expanded in a serious manner Descartes' project of doubting. The result was disastrous: the doctrine of the separation of thought and activity in combination with the results of the new science led to the loss of the very values and qualities for whose preservation the philosophic tradition had, for the most part, been concerned to advance. The Kantian effort to introduce the Non-Spectator Theory of Knowledge to save the certainty destroyed by Hume resulted in an unstable synthesis of the rationalist and empiricist positions. With the collapse of the absoluteness of Newtonian physics, the Kantian project also collapsed—modern science was not absolute and the unchanging categories suddenly became subject to a scientific revolution. Needless to say, the time had come for a reevaluation of the shattered epistemic tradition of the West and of its social consequences.

Dewey's reevaluation of the classic tradition had one central idea: the continuity of thought and practice. Dewey redirected the search for security and knowledge from a "higher" realm isolated from experience to experience itself. Knowledge arose from the need to transform through intelligent activity an insecure situation into a secure one. Knowledge became the result of an activity, a process, because the starting point of knowledge became a reality that was itself process—experience. Since the use of scientific results had led to the disaster of the classic philosophical tradition, Dewey sought the remedy for philosophy's problems in the scientific method. For Dewey, science became the source of our most genuine and authentic knowledge not because the contents of science establish contact with a realm of ultimate reality, but rather because scientific meaning systems best explained the phenomena they sought to investigate and yielded solutions to scientific problems. Here the point must be made clear that Dewey did not seek to enthrone science as the only field in which genuine knowledge was possible but to indicate that it was the only field in which the pragmatic methods of gaining knowledge had been applied and that science was thus the paradigm in method for all other inquiry, including social inquiry. Using the Non-Spectator Theory of Kant, Dewey's view of the continuity of thought and action "installs man, thinking man, within nature."[4] Thus, the metaphysical dualism of the modern era was replaced by the view of man as a part of nature for whom values and qualities emerge from his interaction with nature.

Values emerge from these interactions and become *de jure* values making moral claims once they have been organized by intelligence and tested in experience. A clue to Dewey's social thought is his use of the term "intelligence." He views intelligence not as a thing, as held by the substance philosophies of the past, but as an emergent quality arising from man's interaction with nature. The idea of process permeates

Dewey's use of the terms "nature," "knowledge," "mind," and "intelligence." Darwin's theories contributed to Dewey's strong belief in continuity and process and further strengthened his contention that knowledge was the result of interactions or operations. Because of the Darwinian influence on philosophy, Dewey sees interest shifting "from the wholesale essence back of special changes to the question of how special changes serve and defeat concrete purposes . . . ."[5]

The method that will enable us to focus on the question of how changes affect purposes is the scientific method. In *Freedom and Culture*, Dewey makes the importance of scientific method to social inquiry clear:

> We have been considering science as a body of conclusions. We have ignored science in its quality of an attitude embodied in habitual will to employ certain methods of observation, reflection, and test rather than others. When we look at science from this point of view, the significance of science as a constituent of culture takes on a new color.[6]

The "new color" assumed by science as a part of culture derives from the fact that the scientific spirit sets up a new criterion for knowledge—testing for consequences in experience. Absolute principles and tenets are replaced by working hypotheses.

Thus, Dewey's primary targets in his social thought will be prefabricated solutions to social problems—those solutions that have acquired the label of "ideologies." In his analysis of the epistemic tradition, Dewey highlights several characteristics of the ideological approach to social problems. The approach that separates thought from activity, what I have labeled the ideological approach, is first of all elitist. This characteristic is evident in the Greek world view that contemplation leads to knowledge and that results in the Platonic utopia in which all persons in society are subject to the rule of a small group of elite wise men. In the modern era, the elites will arise in more subtle ways, which will be explored in the next chapter. The second characteristic of this approach is a static character accompanied by a deep hatred for revisionism. For if you once have access to the ultimate Truth and Destiny of Man, how can you tolerate deviations that can serve only to hinder the unfolding of the Truth? The third characteristic of the ideological approach is that it is attractive as a haven offering security during troubled times. Inevitably, social and political thought that is ideological will have an advantage over the pragmatic-scientific approach when groups are faced with new crises. Whether this advantage is real or only apparent and can be overcome must be a question to be investigated by any exploration of the relevance of Dewey's social thought. In addition, the ideological approach is characterized by a reductionist tendency. Dewey uses a tortuous phrase for those theories with the basic tendency to reduce the complex interactions of human nature with the environment to a single principle: "monistic block-universe theor[ies] of social causation."[7]

CHAPTER 2: LIBERALISM AND THE ACTIVIST PHILOSOPHY

The social thought of John Dewey logically originates in his analysis of the history of epistemic issues as briefly outlined in the previous chapter. But in order to understand the background of Dewey's social thought, the immediate tradition from which it historically arises and which it transforms—Anglo-American liberalism—must first be explored.

Dewey's positions have usually been labelled "liberal." Like most political labels, this one, as any historian would readily agree, must first be narrowed. For "liberalism" has been attached to various political movements and positions throughout the history of Western democracies. The political tradition of which Dewey's social thought is a critical development and transformation begins, according to Dewey himself, with the philosophy of John Locke in the time of the Glorious Revolution. The assertion of parliamentary authority in the face of royal absolutist pretensions led to Locke's exposition of a theory of natural rights inhering in the individual. In the introduction to the expanded version of *Reconstruction in Philosophy*, Dewey points to the need for present philosophy to do what "the great doctrines of the past did in and for the cultural media out of which they arose."[8] What Locke's philosophy accomplished was to provide a theoretical framework for the resolution of the controversial social issues of the late seventeenth century. The rise of middle-class groups and the consequent overthrow of royalist pretensions about the workings of the English polity were expressed in Locke's appeal to natural rights that governments were bound to protect, since such rights "belong to individuals prior to political organization of social relations."[9] Thus, with Locke, liberalism arises as a political and social movement concerned with asserting the claims of the individual upon the most powerful social institution—government.

The milieu of this liberalism is then transformed, earlier in England than in America, by the process of industrialization. Typical of the philosophical attraction to the Newtonian model of nature—an attraction resulting from the Greek/Spectator presuppositions about knowledge—is the formulation by Adam Smith of the idea that the unhindered activities of individuals, as discrete units pursuing self-interest, lead to the social equivalent of harmony in the Newtonian universe. In Smith's view, the individual's freedom is justified not only by its status as a Lockean natural right but also as the catalyst of a naturally harmonious mechanism for social prosperity and welfare. In 1776 this economic individualism was well-received in England where small factories were the order of the day—for example, consider the ten-man pin factory discussed by Smith.[10]

As the nineteenth century progressed, gradual industrialization became the Industrial Revolution; and the rising middle classes expanded their power. Bentham's utilitarian approach to the social problems of this time developed the position of Adam Smith on the role of the individual to its logical conclusion. As Dewey points out, for Bentham "not natural rights [as for Locke] but consequences in the lives of individuals are the criteria and measures of policy and judgment."[11]

From the Utilitarians, later liberalism would retain this new type of criterion for policy. The influence of Bentham is justly emphasized by Dewey in *Liberalism and Social Action* for two reasons. First, the new emphasis on consequences provides a closer link between liberalism and the realm of activity when compared to the Lockean state of nature, which is closer to the more metaphysical—and thus more in the Greek epistemic tradition—social philosophy of the continent. In addition, Bentham's school emphasized legal and administrative reforms in response to the consequences of social acts arising in practice. Dewey's emphasis on scientific method has a historic precedent in Bentham's views because these views "greatly weakened the notion that Reason is a remote majestic power that discloses ultimate truths."[12] Reason now becomes a tool in analyzing "concrete situations and in projection of measures for their betterment."[13]

The transition from Locke's natural rights theory to Bentham's utilitarian liberalism is a change that makes Dewey's new liberalism possible in our century [at the time of writing the original essay, the twentieth century but also, in my view, applicable to the twenty-first century]. The change from reference to the metaphysical construct behind natural rights to the Benthamite emphasis on practical activity yielding consequences for individuals allows Dewey to unite pragmatism to the liberal tradition. As a reforming tradition preoccupied with consequences, liberalism as reshaped by the utilitarians is more similar to the pragmatic project of resolving problems than it would be as a static tradition about natural rights.

Yet this *laissez-faire* liberalism was for Dewey the antiquated liberalism which he in fact struggled to discredit. Benthamite liberalism was still working within the Spectator Theory and thus relying on consequences as expressions of an antecedent reality. For these early liberals, the components of antecedent social reality are not the Greek Forms or absolute truths to be grasped by reason, but individuals who in their discreteness as substances were the social atoms of a philosophy deeply influenced by the scientific view of physical reality. In response to his "Newtonian" liberalism, Dewey constructs a new liberal philosophy based on the evolutionary notion of continuity. Rather than discrete units, Dewey emphasizes nature as a process and the individual as being within that process and thus continuous with nature.

These modifications of *laissez-faire* liberalism were first provided, not by Dewey, but by ideas that would at first appear to be completely alien to Dewey's thought: romanticism and idealism.

The English Romantics would react to the materialism and chaos of the new economic individualism by emphasizing the need for sustaining organic relationships among individuals as essential to a society that would preserve true individuality. Wordsworth, in opposition to the impersonal logic of utilitarianism, would seek to enthrone "the sentient, the animal, the vital" as the criteria and guides to action for "a social and political state where these most natural elements can find the satisfaction they demand."[14] Dewey would later make the same point by emphasizing that the values emerging from man's interactions with the environment are not reducible to either purely monetary or scientific categories. Coleridge also protests this reductionism by emphasizing the loss of the qualitative aspect in education and social relations. Dewey succinctly sums up his own criticism of the reductionist tendencies of the empiricists and the utilitarians by pointing out, in the *Quest for Certainty*, that it is absurd to claim that the relations, investigated by science, among qualitative events are more real than the qualitative events themselves.

Thus, to utilitarianism is added a conscientious respect for the need to consider the whole man at all levels of his interaction with nature. For Dewey, this consideration will mean an abiding concern for both the economic and cultural life of the factory worker. Dewey's views on the relation between democracy and culture are tied to his remarkable, because rare, and perceptive emphasis on the need to enable the so-called "masses" to benefit not only from economic democracy but also from cultural democracy.

The final contribution to this evolution of liberalism, as outlined by Dewey in *Liberalism and Social Action*, is idealism's insight that "men are held together by relations . . . [and thus] that the basis of society and state is shared intelligence and purpose . . . ."[15] The underlying basis for Dewey's ability to relate his epistemic reliance on the scientific method with democracy is readily apparent. Democracy, for Dewey, is cooperative and thus becomes the best-suited forum for the application of intelligence, or the scientific method, to social problems. Since scientific results are "the best authenticated knowledge we have," the scientific method is the most effective method of inquiry in the task of converting problematic situations into determinate and harmonious situations.[16] To apply the method of science in social affairs requires a community of free inquiry in which, as John Stuart Mill would say, the truth can emerge from the collision of different ideas. Democracy is the only polity that provides a framework for cooperative sharing of widely divergent ideas in the freedom necessary to nurture creativity. Dewey views democracy much as many view the university as a community of persons with varied backgrounds and interests searching for truth in an atmosphere of freedom.

The liberalism of Dewey is the result of philosophical analysis of the evolution of liberalism in England and America. The individual as the primary social unit, consequences upon individuals as criteria for social policy, all of man's interactions with nature as equally real and relevant, and the application of scientific method as a process of shared intelligence are central concepts in Dewey's social thought. That these ideas are also a litany of the evolution of liberalism indicates the importance of the tradition from which Dewey saw his own social philosophy arising. The accusation by the Marxist critic George Novack that pragmatism lacks a sense of steadfast principles and is merely a label for contradictory political opportunism is clearly based on ignorance of the dialectic evident between the history of liberalism and Dewey's social thought.

The point must be made, in order to preempt such criticism, that to emphasize scientific method in place of a noumenal realm of changeless forms is not to desert ideals but to redefine them. No longer are ideals to be seen as objects or things apart from experience—this view would be the substance philosophy of much of Western thought. For the pragmatist, ideals become a "collection of imagined possibilities" that lead to action that seeks to remedy social problems.[17] The pragmatic approach does not ignore ideals but is, in fact, more loyal to ideals than the classic tradition. The classical tradition in philosophy separated ideals from experience and thus contributed to the substitution of improvised and lesser ideals for those ideals removed from human reach by traditional metaphysics. In other words, the separation of ideals from experience leads to a Machiavellian prince. Dewey, on the other hand, sees ideals as the starting-points for attacking social problems; ideals direct us to problems and move us to action to resolve the problematic situation.

Dewey's place in the liberal tradition is not that of a passive receiver of a glorious heritage but that of a critical user and synthesizer of liberalism's groping toward the destruction of the separation of thought and practice. In *New Studies in the Philosophy of John Dewey*, Charles Frankel warns the student of Dewey's social thought with the following: "Dewey's philosophy is distorted when it is treated as an American reply to Marx, or as an episode in the history of ideological confrontation between liberalism and Marxism."[18] This warning serves to make explicit the danger in trivializing Dewey's thought by making it too "American" or "liberal." The writings of Dewey serve to make one point clear: Dewey's thought is obviously influenced by the American and liberal experiences; but the basic approaches, with which he would later reinterpret the American and liberal experience, arose from his critical analysis of the entire philosophical tradition of the West. Consideration of the epistemic and metaphysical issues of philosophy led to Dewey's pragmatic approach to social problems—not simply the bare empirical history of liberalism. The wider concept of the continuity of thought and action led to the pragmatic renewal of the liberal tradition—a renewal that was at the same time a revolutionary break with the previous philosophical frameworks of Locke and Bentham, which were rooted in the Spectator Theory of Knowledge.

◆ ◆ ◆

CHAPTER 3: IDEOLOGY, VALUE, AND THE ACTIVIST PHILOSOPHY

To place the pragmatic approach to social philosophy in its epistemic and historical context depicts only the framework within which to evaluate its relevance to man's social problems. Dewey's social philosophy must answer to the criticisms of others who also endeavor to come to terms with the dark areas of social life and with the ethical ends which are an inseparable part of both social reform and revolution. Before proceeding it must be made clear that this evaluation of Dewey's philosophy is not in contradiction with Dewey's reproach of social philosophers who weave intricate dialectical webs that ignore actual problems and actual suffering. The deductive process of exploring the ramifications and intricacies of Dewey's social thought seeks to "define, delimit, purify and set in order the conceptions through which this enriching and directive operation, (i.e. problem-solving) is carried on . . . ."[19] The quote is Dewey's, and the message is that theoretical exploration is necessary in order to make application possible and meaningful. For Dewey, this practical version of theorizing mediates between problematic situations in the same way that the scientist seeks to produce a hypothesis that will bring present knowledge to bear on new problems. This functional perfecting of knowledge and hypotheses is Dewey's answer to the traditional metaphysical speculation centered on static and self-sufficient abstractions.

The ideological approach is proud of such static and isolated abstractions because these abstractions are believed to provide access to the "real" workings of social life. But from where do ideologies derive the mandate of absolutism? The mandate arises from the process of abstraction itself. What then keeps pragmatism, which like other philosophic thought engages in abstraction, from claiming such a mandate? The answer brings us back to Dewey's view of abstractions as working hypotheses that become knowledge only after embodiment in activities and testing of consequences. The ideological approach, on the contrary, goes to abstraction as a hermit goes to the desert: to find life where there is in fact no life.

The primary ideological force in the world today, as in Dewey's lifetime, is nationalism. Surprise may arise at this slighting of Marxism. Nevertheless, Marxism will be acknowledged later; nationalism is considered first because many Marxist acts in the world today are best understood through a consideration of nationalism. The ideology of nationalism exhibits the elitism of other ideologies in its cult of hero-worship. Nationalism sees the individual as experiencing freedom in the state's action and glorification. This spectacle is best exemplified in the propaganda of past and present totalitarian states that promise liberation from troubles to their peoples only through submission to their absolute authority. The hero becomes the symbol through which the submissive individual can vicariously participate in a purely abstract freedom.

Nationalists would decry the scientific method of Dewey's thought as aimless and uninspiring. The basic criticism is that the pragmatic approach ignores the frustration and alienation inherent in individual existence by not allowing the individual to leap into the arms of the state cult.

This criticism has a wider set of proponents. Both Marxists and conservatives would repeat the same criticism from different standpoints. Both would say with George Novack that if "each concrete case may be a law unto itself, no general rules govern events and no definite principles can be reliable guides to action."[20] For the Marxist, the missing guide is dialectical materialism; for the conservative, it is the hierarchical nature of human society. Even the politically liberal theist can join the chorus: Dewey provides no ends or purposes for individual reforming action.

This criticism is threatening for Dewey's position because Dewey assigned to himself the task of providing an alternative to the valueless reductionism and commercialization of American life. He consistently exposed the contradiction between a way of life that was the embodiment of economic determinism and the ideals held by the American nation.[21] If Dewey cannot answer these critics, then his social philosophy has failed to stand for the continuity of thought and activity he envisioned.

What is the place of values and ends in Dewey's social thought? In order to answer his critics, Dewey's treatment of values must at the same time reject the economic determinism and the useless ideals of American social life: "When we take means for ends we indeed fall into moral materialism. But when we take ends without regard to means we degenerate into sentimentalism."[22] Thus, values will point beyond the present problematic situation and yet be tied to action; and Dewey, consequently, defines values as imagined possibilities that lead to practical activity.[23] In order to have intelligent action, or reconstruction, in society, ideals must be rejuvenated and created. Dewey does not deny the worth of ideals or man's need for them. He treats ideals as prerequisites for reconstruction and thus as inherent parts of the pragmatic method. The point that Dewey strives to emphasize is that ideals are beneficial only to the extent that they are tied to intelligent operations.

What then are these ideals? The ideals that are tied to intelligent operations are values in the literal sense of the term:

the principles men have found, in experience, to be conducive to their increase in happiness. But care must be taken not to see this statement as simply putting Dewey in the utilitarian camp. That there are significant similarities between Bentham and Dewey is not surprising; we have already examined the liberal background to Dewey's thought. The distinction between the role played by happiness in utilitarianism and that which it plays in Dewey's pragmatism lies in the different use to which the ideal of happiness is put by each one in the resolution of social problems. The utilitarian approach treats static happiness as the product of static individuals by which to evaluate all our actions. The practical effect of this approach is the tendency to ignore the particular and variable factors that make every judgment's context unique. In other words, situations may arise in which obvious values—obvious that is to the common-sense person who refuses to be an ideologue—are dismissed for the sake of "the greatest happiness for the greatest number." This distortion of specific situations by a general formula is the ideological approach in its essence. On the other hand, for Dewey happiness would be a general and descriptive term that refers to the consequences that have been demonstrated by past experience to advance the fulfillment of mankind's needs. "Happiness" humbly assumes its functional role of referring to the general characteristics of specific activities, not of replacing those activities in a calculus of utility.[24] Dewey, consequently, posits many ends rather than one; and these ends become "modifiers of action in special cases."[25] Ends are multiple and specific because actions are "always specific, concrete, individualized, unique."[26] The listing of moral goods thus exists for the purpose of enhancing activity that resolves the problematic and has the role of suggesting an approach to the analysis of a problematic situation; moral goods are thus simply "tools of insight" aimed at the indeterminate.[27]

The realization that moral ends play a strong role in the scientific approach to social problems thus rejects the accusation that Dewey advocates a method that ignores the fundamental values of a reflective moral tradition. An approach that does seek to separate rational ends from actions is that of David Hume. Hume repeatedly points out that reason because inactive "can never be the source of so active a principle as conscience, or a sense of morals."[28] For Hume, the mover to moral action is passion. This artificial distinction arises from the fact that Hume is working within a framework that separates thought from activity by making interpretation subsequent to "raw" sensation. Dewey's approach, on the other hand, sees a continuity between thought and action in which the existential need for action arises with deliberate thought that identifies the problematic, thus forging an intimate relationship between reason and action. Like Dewey, Hume sees the inadequacy of static reason in moving us to action. Yet Hume erroneously replaces reason by the passions because he himself accepts reason as a static entity. Dewey redefines reason as intelligent behavior; intelligence becomes "a shorthand designation for . . . methods," not for a substance.[29] Consequently, Dewey has no need to call for a moral realm divorced from reason; such a stand avoids the endless contradictions and controversies engendered by an absolute separation of the components of what, in reality, is a continuous process.

But if ideals are part of a "super-empirical" realm as in ideologies, the practical result is usually the opposite of the ideals. This self-contradiction inherent in the ideological approach exists because, sooner or later, practical decisions must be made and action taken even by the adherents of the most impassioned ideological reverie. How can a super-empirical set of absolute ideals pretending to provide access to an ultimate reality become hypotheses of practical action? They cannot—thus, we have the improvisation by an elite of the working hypotheses needed by experience. Ideologies make their dogmas public but leave the actual guides of operations in the bureaucratic labyrinth. The resulting hypotheses are then subject to all the whims of individual delusion, ambition, and hatred; they become the personal products of personal fiefdoms. Instead of minded behavior, the citizens of ideological-totalitarian nations are left to deal with government actions based on the goals of a power-hungry, and often paranoid, faction. On the other hand, the pragmatic approach is straightforward from the very beginning of any discussion about ideals: ideals are not a sort of Jacob's ladder to higher realms but rather creative meaning systems that stimulate directed activities. The workings of totalitarian government point to what Dewey would call the intellectualist fallacy of ideology: that the most unchanging and thus most knowable is the most real. Ideologues thus believe that their dialectical edifices are the most real and consequently are exempt from the judgments of experience. This fallacy reduces ideals to empty forms that can give the individual a comforting feeling, but the price is the abolition of the influence of ideals in everyday life.

This paralysis of ideals can result in ironic social arrangements. In the United States Dewey directed attention to the way in which individualism of the *laissez-faire* variety led to the crushing of the dignity and lives of millions of individuals. The old liberalism elevated individualism to an absolute to which all social arrangements must yield. Once again, the revisionism of experimentation and growth is thwarted. The resulting picture is one of a minority of prosperous individuals calling for the permanent economic and cultural disenfranchisement of a vastly greater number of individuals in the name of the sacredness of individual dignity.

In addition to accusing Dewey's pragmatic approach of deserting values or ideals, others have also criticized his treatment of science as a disembodied force that has no relation to political realities.[30] The Marxist, of course, bases his criticism on the fact that Dewey ignores the class conflict underlying all social turmoil. On the other side of the spectrum, theologian Reinhold Niebuhr ridicules Dewey's appeal for the application of scientific method to social problems by saying that Dewey:

seeks a secure place for disinterested intelligence

> above the flux of process; and finds it in "organized co-operative inquiry." Not a suspicion draws upon Professor Dewey that no possible "organized inquiry" can be as transcendent over the historical conflicts of interest as it ought to be to achieve the disinterested intelligence which he attributes to it. Every such "organized inquiry" must have its own social locus.[31]

In other words, Niebuhr accuses Dewey of naively forgetting about the inevitable bias and imperfection that taint even the most creative human efforts and, as a result, sees Dewey's reliance on cooperative inquiry as unrealistic optimism. What then are Professor Dewey's expectations? In 1920, Dewey foreshadowed Niebuhr's question by advocating meliorism, over optimism, as "the belief that the specific conditions which exist at any one moment, be they comparatively bad or comparatively good, in any event may be bettered . . . It rouses confidence and a reasonable hopefulness as optimism does not."[32] Dewey believes that some progress can be made, and as a pragmatist Dewey adopts the attitude toward the possibility of such progress that will have the strongest effect in encouraging such endeavors. Thus, Dewey rejects both optimism and pessimism as paralyzing the efforts to remedy social ills, the former because of self-satisfaction and the latter because of despair.

Such criticism like that of Niebuhr usually arises because of the mistaken impression of critics that Dewey is always pointing to science as the cure for social problems. A more accurate statement of Dewey's position is that he is speaking about the *method* found in scientific inquiry as an approach for social reconstruction. The confusion is also abetted by the consistent attempts to place Dewey in the category labelled "rationalist-optimist" rather than to understand Dewey's efforts in the light of the liberal tradition of hard-headed gradual reform. Examination of this tradition is a better guide than instinct as to what Dewey expected of "cooperative inquiry."

CHAPTER 4: DEMOCRACY, SCIENTIFIC METHOD, AND THE ACTIVIST PHILOSOPHY

This reliance on "cooperative inquiry" causes many to accuse Dewey of a naïve rationalistic faith that is a relic of the Enlightenment, irrelevant to the experience of this century [twentieth century at the time of writing]. The Enlightenment becomes a label of reproach in this context because it becomes a code word for faith in reason as a panacea. In fact, the Enlightenment tradition has a positive side with which Dewey agrees: the attempt to break out of archaic dogmas in order to resolve social problems. The easy optimism of the Enlightenment—the "negative side" of this era—becomes in Dewey's thought a determination to recognize and face problems, not to dismiss them with euphemisms.

Dewey's belief in democracy as the social vehicle for a wider application of the scientific method is not a delusion. There are specific reasons why democracy holds the best hope for the adoption of a scientific approach to social problems. The method of democratic policy-making is the best approximation in the social sphere to the scientific method. Why?

A democracy upholds free inquiry and free expression of the results of such inquiry. One of the best presentations of this fundamental part of the democratic experience is expressed by

John Stuart Mill as follows:

> Truth, in the practical concerns of life, is so much a question of the reconciling and combining of opposites, that very few have minds sufficiently capacious and impartial to make the adjustment with an approach to correctness, and it has to be made by the rough process of a struggle between combatants fighting under hostile banners.[33]

This clash of ideas resulting from free inquiry and free speech is the most efficient method of seeking truth: any approach other than that of toleration assumes, as Mill points out, infallibility.[34] Such a view of how truth arises and is found is furthest from the accusation of a "naïve belief in reason." For Dewey, a naïve belief in reason is a belief in reason as a key to ideological dogmas; belief in reason as emerging from planned and directed activities testing working hypotheses is not naïve. The stance of both Mill and Dewey is that of the realist who is well aware of the powerful bias toward self-interest inherent in human nature. Thus, democracy with its toleration for divergent views becomes the best way to identify truth in view of the human tendency to reason under a class bias.

Democracy's freedom of thought is thus a response to the challenge of social life, not a retreat. Once again, the determination to identify and encounter problems regardless of their venerable status has been mistaken for foolish optimism. To restate Winston Churchill's well-known dictum about democracy, democracy is the best of many imperfect methods that seek to deal with the complexities of social life. Dewey's analysis of past approaches to social problems, in addition, demonstrates that democracy is the best method because most of the other imperfect methods have sought to approach the problems of human life by denigrating the primary social tasks of human life.

Unlike the ideological approach, the democratic approach, like the scientific method, welcomes revision and is free of the need to destroy heretics. Revision is welcome because knowledge is seen as arising from experimentation in experience, not from the ideological purity of an enlightened minority. Dewey's thought emphasizes the democratic aspect of knowledge itself by constantly treating knowledge as public and social. Dewey sees democracy, not as the result of atomic individuals pursuing their self-interest in a world of perfect competition, but as the result of social and public cooperation that uses free inquiry to resolve problematic situations. Freedom of thought is not embraced as an end in itself, as a dogma; but it is embraced as a tool needed by the community to meet the needs of its members. This pragmatic view of democracy is another example of Dewey's transformation of the philosophical framework of liberalism. The old liberalism of unimpeded individual freedom became a new ideology for business interests; the theories of Bentham became useful excuses in the corporate age for the greed of the owners of the means of production and for the accompanying abuse of workers. Again, Dewey's view of the continuity between man and nature and of the importance of man's interactions with his culture rebuffs the attempt to use liberal ideas for inhuman ends. Reduction of social life to a valueless, and thus inhuman, level results when the individualism of an earlier time is transferred to a corporate age in which such individualism becomes a synonym for social Darwinism. Dewey's view of values as emerging from man's interactions with nature is in direct opposition to those ideologies that portray values as emerging from an absolute dogmatic interpretation of social life and remaining in the dogmatic realm.

In the case of the earlier liberalism, the individual "was a Newtonian atom having only external time and space relations to other individuals, save that each social atom was equipped with inherent freedom"; Dewey's response to this absolutization of a working hypothesis is the logical extension of his epistemic views.[35] In the article "The Future of Liberalism," Dewey, in writing about the new liberalism, lists the various hallmarks of a new approach to knowledge: "[that] an individual is nothing fixed . . . [use of] the idea of historical relativity . . . experimental procedure . . . [and] realistic study of existing conditions"; and, finally, Dewey declares how "ideas and theory must be taken as methods of action tested and continuously revised by the consequences they produce in actual conditions."[36]

Yet democracy's experimental character poses the danger, mentioned earlier, that in a world of crisis and uncertainty it will lose frightened individuals to the security offered by ideology. How can democracy respond to this practical danger of losing its participants to dogmatism?

The new liberalism responds by treating the individual as more than just a rational creature, by taking the individual as Unamuno describes him: "The man of flesh and bone; the man who is born, suffers, and dies—above all, who dies; the man who eats and drinks and plays and sleeps and thinks and wills; the man who is seen and heard; the brother, the real brother."[37] Democracy must retain the allegiance and participation of such men. The problem of voter apathy and the breakdown of party discipline in the United States have arisen in part because of the materialistic [i.e., consumerist] philosophy that relegates the individual to a narrow self-interest. The vitality of social community is thus lost; and faith in democracy gives way to cynicism toward helpless institutions and politicians. Dewey's early exposure to Hegelianism alerted him to the tendency of older liberalism to ignore the "man of flesh and bone" and his concerns. Dewey sees true individual dignity as something achieved with "the aid and support of conditions, cultural and physical, including in 'cultural' economic, legal, and political institutions as well as science and art."[38] Dewey makes equal access to cultural life an explicit part of the program of the new liberalism. Culture, or social arrangements, becomes an important factor in the reconstruction of democracy as a result of the crisis caused by what Dewey terms "cultural lag"—the failure of traditional and customary modes of response to keep up with technological advances. Dewey, thus, directly attacks the problem of apathy so evident in American democracy when he states how:

> No estimate of the effects of culture upon the elements that make up freedom begins to be adequate that does not take into account the moral and religious splits that are found in our very makeup as persons. The problem of genuine democracy cannot be successfully dealt with . . . save as we create intellectual and moral integration out of present disordered conditions.[39]

Another crucial issue for democracy and Dewey's liberalism is the issue of elitism: in spite of Dewey's love for democracy, is there not a strong case for the need to nourish a strong elite in order to ensure progress in the resolution of social issues? Is Dewey's democratic fervor the quaint nostalgia of a small-town New Englander or a relevant part of a pragmatic approach to the future?

The case for elites is strongly stated by the Spanish philosopher José Ortega y Gasset as follows:

> For there is no doubt that the most radical division that it is possible to make of humanity is that which splits it into two classes of creatures: those who make great demands upon themselves, piling up difficulties and duties; and those who demand nothing special of themselves, but for whom to live is to be every moment what they already are, without imposing on themselves any effort towards perfection; mere buoys that float on the waves.[40]

The latter class consists of the "masses"; the first class is the elite. This description of the human situation cannot be dismissed lightly in Dewey's social thought. Dewey justifies democracy because of its application of scientific method to public problems. But, in fact, from where does democracy derive its momentum, if not from its own elites? An activist citizen like Dewey, rather than the member of a mob, makes democracy progressive and vital.

Dewey's response to this issue is evident throughout his writings and lectures: we must engage in building a new "elite." Obviously, Dewey believes in the values cultivated by elites. Why else would he castigate those with access to the cultural resources of a society for not sharing those resources with the worker, the farmhand, and the small businessman? Unlike Ortega, Dewey does not see in the continued existence of elites an absolute and static norm by which to judge the vitality of current societies. Dewey sees the existence of elites as a problematic situation because the cultural resources of an entire tradition are subject to the egotistic manipulation of a few who happen to be members of the same social class. This monopoly of the sources of knowledge leads to control of the rest of society by leaders who are master demagogues, whether they are using nationalistic or religious sectarianism as their road to greater power and prestige or simply to preserve the status quo. As a result, the activist philosophy of Dewey seeks to increase the size of the elite in order to bring about its self-destruction as a privileged minority. The enlightened few of traditional society must become the enlightened majority of a new democratic society in order for the "man of flesh and bone" to be free from the tempting, but ultimately destructive, security of totalitarian ideologies.

◆ ◆ ◆

CHAPTER 5: THE ACTIVIST PHILOSOPHY AND THE CURRENT SITUATION

The goal of economic and cultural democracy is as elusive today as it was in Dewey's lifetime. The political arena—which is the crucial battleground for a social philosophy—is as muddled with ideological myths of both the right and the left as ever. The activist philosophy of John Dewey is, as the name implies, concerned with action. But can intellectual agendas and experiments in social and educational psychology suffice to bring about the transformation of the Great Society into the Great Community promoted by Dewey as the goal of his social thought? The answer is "no." because social transformation becomes a practical possibility only when a political mandate has been achieved through the workings of political democracy and the mass media. The attempts by well-intentioned teachers to reform curricula have been attempts to create individuals for a different society than we now have. As a result, students become experimental subjects guided by an educational philosophy that is rejected by the archaic individualistic and capitalistic philosophy of wider society. In other words, the lesson of social reform efforts in the past is clear: a political consensus for reform must be created simultaneously with efforts at underlying social reconstruction, or else those efforts at social reconstruction will become bearers of the stigma of being unrealistic failures at the hands of a society still controlled by, and still judging with, prescientific and feudal habits.

Dewey's social thought must enter the realm of political action in order for an adequate test of its consequences in experience to become a reality. In a political democracy in which public opinion is already powerful, the challenge is, as Dewey points out, to transform that public opinion:

> Today the judgments popularly formed on political matters are so important, in spite of all factors to the contrary, that there is an enormous premium upon all methods which affect their formation. The smoothest road to control of political conduct is by control of opinion.[41]

Dewey himself was a life-long defender of democratic causes through his writings and protests. Education is the word used by Dewey to describe this transformation of a public at the mercy of the greed and class bias of a few into an attentive and politically mature public that is aware of democracy as both a political *and* social undertaking. In Deweyian language the goal of education is to prepare "masses who shall form a community of directed thought and emotion in spite of being the masses."[42]

But this education must not be limited to the schoolhouse; otherwise, we are failing to make use of the media technology that is a powerful tool for the formation of community in a large and culturally diverse nation. Transformation of social habits must begin with rallying of a majority to the cause of this transformation. Just as the industrial capitalists transformed feudal society into a corporate society by exerting their influence in the political realm, true democrats must begin the construction of a vocal political consensus that will make political machinery the servant of the vision of a Great and Democratic Community.

Dewey's social thought provides contemporary Americans with a philosophical framework for intelligent political action. To use

William James' terminology, Dewey's faith in democracy is a live hypothesis for Americans—probably more so than for other democratic nations whose traditions and customs are less pioneer and more feudal than our own. Political action founded on Dewey's democratic faith is intelligent to the extent to which it follows the pattern of Dewey's social philosophy by articulating well-considered goals, by being conscious of its liberal heritage, by appealing to the whole man, and by maintaining its loyalty to a democratic vision in which individual dignity becomes the rationale for equal individual participation in political, economic, and cultural life.

The foe of a pragmatic reconstruction of American life is a politically powerful beneficiary of the traditional separation of thought from action. This foe is the same enemy of all democratic reform: an elite adept at profiting from the toil of the majority without sharing the fruits of that toil on the basis of equality. Equality is "not a natural possession but is a fruit of the community when its action is directed by its character as a community."[43] Participatory democracy is the clear political call sounded by Dewey that is aimed at ideology and commercialism as the artifacts to be replaced by the experience and human values of citizens that have been living, not in a world of perfect market competition among many sellers and producers, but in a world of powerful corporate institutions.[44] Dewey's social philosophy will find its vindication only in that new democratic transformation.

◆ ◆ ◆

NOTES

[1] Frankel, Charles, "John Dewey's Social Philosophy," in *New Studies in the Philosophy of John Dewey*, ed. Steven M. Cahn (Hanover, New Hampshire: The University Press of New England, 1977), p. 5.

[2] Macpherson, C. B., *The Life and Times of Liberal Democracy* (Oxford: Oxford University Press, 1977), p. 76.

[3] *Life and Times*, p. 76.

[4] Dewey, John, *The Quest for Certainty* (1929; reprint, New York: G. P. Putnam's Sons, 1979), p. 211.

[5] Frankel, p. 44.

[6] Dewey, John, *Freedom and Culture* (1939; reprint, New York: G. P. Putnam's Sons, 1979), p. 145.

[7] Dewey, *Freedom and Culture*, p. 88. The original "theory" has been changed to "theories."

[8] Dewey, John, *Reconstruction in Philosophy* (1920; reprint, Boston: Beacon Press, enlarged edition, 1948), p. viii.

[9] Dewey, John, *Liberalism and Social Action* (1935; reprint, New York: G. P. Putnam's Sons, 1980), p. 4. The basic historical outline used in this chapter is based on chapter one of *Liberalism and Social Action*.

[10] Heilbroner, Robert L., *The Worldly Philosophers*, 5th ed. (New York: Simon and Schuster, 1980), p. 59.

[11] Dewey, *Liberalism and Social Action*, p. 17.

[12] Dewey, *Liberalism and Social Action*, p. 20.

[13] Dewey, *Liberalism and Social Action*, p. 20.

[14] Brinton, Crane, *Political Ideas of the English Romanticists* (London: Oxford University Press, 1926), p. 63.

[15] Dewey, *Liberalism and Social Action*, p. 25.

[16] Dewey, *Freedom and Culture*, p. 138.

[17] Dewey, *Reconstruction*, p. 118.

[18] Frankel, *New Studies*, p. 40.

[19] Dewey, *Reconstruction*, p. 151.

[20] Novack, George, *Pragmatism versus Marxism: An Appraisal of John Dewey's Philosophy* (New York: Pathfinder Press, 1975), p. 83.

[21] Dewey, John, *Individualism Old and New* (1929; reprint, New York: G. P. Putnam's Sons, 1962), Ch. 1.

[22] Dewey, *Reconstruction*, p. 73.

[23] Dewey, *Reconstruction*, p. 118.

[24] See Chapter 5 of Dewey's *Experience and Nature* (1929; reprint, New York: Dover Publications, 1958), for his discussion of language, meaning, and nominalism, especially pp. 184-185.

[25] Dewey, *Reconstruction*, p. 167.

[26] Dewey, *Reconstruction*, p. 167.

[27] Dewey, *Reconstruction*, p. 169.

[28] Hume, David, *A Treatise of Human Nature*, ed. L. A. Selby-Bigge and P. H. Nidditch, 2nd ed. (London: Oxford University Press, 1978), p. 458.

[29] Dewey, *Reconstruction*, p. viii.

[30] Frankel, pp. 10-11.

[31] Niebuhr, Reinhold, *The Nature and Destiny of Man* (New York: Charles Scribner's Sons, 1941), I, p. 111.

[32] Dewey, *Reconstruction*, p. 178.

[33] Mill, John Stuart, "On Liberty," in *Utilitarianism, On Liberty, and Considerations on Representative Government*, ed. H. B. Acton (New York: E. P. Dutton Co., 1972), p. 107.

[34] Mill, John Stuart, *Utilitarianism*, p. 79.

[35] Dewey, John, "The Future of Liberalism," *The Journal of Philosophy*, Vol. XXXII, No. 9 (1955); rpt. in *Communism, Fascism, and Democracy: Theoretical Foundations*, ed. Carl Cohen, 2nd ed. (New York: Random House, 1972), p. 497.

[36] Dewey, "The Future of Liberalism," pp. 496-499.

[37] Unamuno, Miguel de, *Tragic Sense of Life*, trans. J. E. Crawford Flitch (1921; reprint, New York: Dover Publications, 1954), p. 1.

[38] Dewey, "The Future of Liberalism," p. 498.

[39] Dewey, *Freedom and Culture*, p. 49.

[40] Ortega y Gasset, José, *The Revolt of the Masses*, trans. anonymous (1932; reprint, New York: W. W. Norton & Co., 1957), p. 15.

[41] Dewey, John, *The Public and Its Problems* (1927; reprint, Chicago: The Swallow Press, 1954), p. 182.

[42] Dewey, John, "American Education and Culture," in *Character and Events*, ed. Joseph Ratner (New York: Henry Holt & Co., 1929), pp. 498-503; rpt. in *John Dewey on Education*, ed. Reginald D. Archambault, Phoenix Edition (Chicago: The University of Chicago Press, 1974), p. 292.

[43] Dewey, *The Public and Its Problems*, p. 151.

[44] See Dewey, John, "Pragmatic America," *The New Republic*, April 12, 1922; rpt. in *Characters and Events*, ed. Joseph Ratner (New York: Henry Holt & Co., 1929), II, p. 547.

ABOUT THE AUTHOR

Oswald Sobrino

Oswald Sobrino wrote this essay on John Dewey as an undergraduate at Loyola University New Orleans in 1983. He had Dr. Sandra B. Rosenthal, a scholar of American Pragmatism, as an honors program philosophy teacher whose excellent instruction made this essay possible. He has now published this essay after almost forty years and after obtaining his Ph.D. in Latin and Roman Studies from the University of Florida. He has taught at the college level for many years.